HOW
TO BE
AWESOME

SOPHIE GOLDING

HOW TO BE AWESOME

An Hachette UK Company
www.hachette.co.uk

Vie Books, an imprint of Summersdale Publishers Ltd
Part of Octopus Publishing Group Limited
Carmelite House
50 Victoria Embankment
LONDON
EC4Y 0DZ
UK

www.summersdale.com

Printed and bound in China

ISBN: 978-1-78783-531-3

Substantial discounts on bulk quantities of Summersdale books are available to corporations, professional associations and other organizations. For details contact general enquiries: telephone: +44 (0) 1243 771107 or email: enquiries@summersdale.com.

CONTENTS

INTRODUCTION

Well hello there, awesome person. Thanks for stopping by. You must be here because at some point you've wondered, why settle for OK when you could be awesome? But what does being awesome even mean, anyway? Taken literally, "awesome" is defined as extremely impressive or daunting; inspiring awe. Informally, it means extremely good, or excellent. More importantly, what does being awesome mean to you?

Being awesome is about showing up as your best self every day. It's finding the positives in every situation, even when things go wrong. It's being an amazing friend, sibling or spouse. It's about knowing your flaws and owning them – embracing your flawesome self. It's about having fun, making the most of life and just, you know, being generally cool and good to have around.

If you're ready to bring awesomeness to all levels of your life, read on for inspiring tips and quotations to set you on your way.

CHAPTER ONE

YOU ARE AWESOME

The good news is that you are already awesome – you just need to realize it! Now the journey continues by accepting yourself for who you are, embracing your flaws and individuality, and becoming confident being you. Awesomeness is whatever you define it as, and perhaps you already have a good idea of what it means to you. Look inside and around you, and you'll recognize that many things about your self and your life are awesome. Once you've reminded yourself of how great you are, you'll be better placed to share your awesomeness with the world.

WHAT DOES AWESOMENESS MEAN TO YOU?

To find the answer, start by looking around you. There are bound to be some people in your life who you think are pretty wonderful. But what is it about them that makes them great? Think about any particular behaviours or habits that demonstrate their brilliance, then create a mood board to group all your ideas together. This can take any form you like – for example, a scrapbook-style collage with colourful labels, or a spider diagram in your journal. The mood board can be a work in progress, as you refine your concept of what makes a person awesome, and you can use it to work on bringing these qualities to the fore in your life.

YOUR BODY IS AWESOME

The world is full of conflicting messages about bodies – what's beautiful and what's not – but really there is only one simple thing you need to remember: learn to accept your body the way it is right now and love it for what it is. Your body is the vessel that carries you through life and allows you to have so many wonderful experiences. So focus on what your body can do instead of how it looks. Have you ever thought about how incredible it is, the way the body heals if you accidentally cut yourself? Or all the things your body does automatically without you even thinking about doing them – like sleeping, digesting your food and breathing? Or the way it allows you to taste, smell and feel pleasure? Each morning, make a point of noting one thing that your body can do and spend some time in quiet reflection expressing gratitude for it.

IT'S WHAT'S
INSIDE THAT
COUNTS:
NOW LET
IT SHINE FOR
ALL TO SEE.

TO ACHIEVE GREATNESS,
START WHERE YOU ARE,
USE WHAT YOU HAVE AND
DO WHAT YOU CAN.

ARTHUR ASHE

DO IT LIKE YOU MEAN IT

Have confidence in your abilities. Whatever challenge you are facing, act with the belief that you will succeed. For example, if you are getting up early on a Saturday morning to do a 5k run, visualize yourself crossing the finish line and going for a healthy breakfast with friends afterward. Or if you have a job interview, walk in there picturing yourself already confidently doing the job. By setting your intentions in this way, you will go into whatever you want to tackle in life with a clear head, undistracted by any negative self-talk.

YOU'VE GOT THIS.

FORGET ABOUT THE REST

We each have our own ways of being awesome, so comparisons are ultimately meaningless. Having said that, comparing yourself to others is only human, so it's a good idea to work on some strategies to minimize this unhelpful behaviour. Figure out what your triggers are, then try to avoid or at least limit your exposure to them. For example, if seeing other people's posts about their engagement/new job/amazing tropical holiday on social media makes you feel envious, consider deleting certain apps from your phone to prevent bouts of scrolling whenever you pick it up. Focus on your own goals and progress and take life at your own pace – never mind what everyone else is doing.

CARE LESS ABOUT WHAT OTHERS THINK

You only get one life, and it's up to you how you live it. Other people's thoughts and opinions, whether real or imagined, can only harm us if we let them. So if it's cold outside, you need to pop to the corner shop and you want to go in your unicorn onesie to stay toasty, go for it!

LOVE BEING YOU

Take some time out to think about all the things that make you who you are. Jot down a list of anything that comes to mind – whether it's the fact that you're great at sport, that you are clumsy when tired, that you love animals or are afraid of the dark. Do this with honesty and without judgement and include everything that you think of, even perceived weaknesses. These are the things that make you awesome and uniquely you.

"

YOU ARE VALUABLE
JUST BECAUSE YOU EXIST.
NOT BECAUSE OF WHAT
YOU DO OR WHAT YOU
HAVE DONE, BUT SIMPLY
BECAUSE YOU ARE.

MAX LUCADO

IF YOU ARE ALWAYS TRYING TO BE NORMAL

YOU WILL NEVER KNOW HOW AMAZING YOU CAN BE.

MAYA ANGELOU

HAVE AN AWESOMENESS MANTRA

Write down a statement declaring your awesomeness. This could be related to something specific you are awesome at ("I am an awesome friend!") or a more general thought ("I have everything I need to realize my dreams"). Stand in front of a mirror and repeat your awesomeness mantra to yourself whenever you need the reminder.

IF YOU'RE
SEARCHING
FOR AWESOME,
THE ONLY
PLACE YOU
NEED TO LOOK
IS INSIDE.

AWARD YOURSELF AN AWESOMENESS BADGE

All too often in life we achieve one goal and move straight to working on the next one. But it's important to take time out to celebrate your successes, even the little ones along the way. Next time you tick something off your list of goals, celebrate by awarding yourself a badge – this could be in the literal sense, with a gold star or a badge that says "Awesome", or by buying yourself a treat or setting aside some time to enjoy an activity with friends. As well as celebrating, take some quiet time to pause and reflect on the hard work that got you there and any negative feelings you may have had along the way ("I'll never make it!" or "This is too hard!"). The next time you are working on something and similar negative thoughts crop up, remind yourself that it's part of the process and you'll get through it, as you have done before.

PRACTISE
KINTSUGI

Kintsugi is the Japanese art of reassembling broken pottery using powdered gold to highlight the break lines. The repaired pot, with its network of fine gold lines, is more beautiful than the original. None of us are perfect. All of us fall apart at some point in life. When we get up and pull ourselves back together, we are never quite the same as before. We are something stronger, something more. Like the golden filigree of lines on a pot mended with *kintsugi*, your flaws and past mistakes are what make you unique. Embrace them and the beauty that they bring to your life.

SELF-TRUST IS THE FIRST SECRET TO SUCCESS.

RALPH WALDO EMERSON

THINK KIND THOUGHTS

If you think kindly of others, you are more likely to think kindly of yourself – to accept yourself for who you are in all your flawesome glory. Practise this next time you are out people-watching at a cafe or on your daily commute. If you catch yourself thinking something negative about a person you see ("That woman's outfit is so last season" or "That man is so wrinkly"), turn it around into a compliment ("That woman has a fantastic haircut" or "That man has a lovely smile"). Maybe even give the person you are looking at a friendly smile. Now think of something positive about yourself that others may notice as they pass you – perhaps you have a new hat you're particularly proud of, or you have great posture and walk with confidence.

YOU WERE BORN TO BE AWESOME, NOT PERFECT.

CELEBRATE YOUR STRENGTHS

Make a list of your good qualities. For example: "I am generous", "I make a mean lasagne", or "I am determined." Write each one on a sticky note and put them up around your home. They will serve as timely, cheerful reminders of how awesome you are.

FIND OUT WHO YOU ARE
AND DO IT ON PURPOSE.

DOLLY PARTON

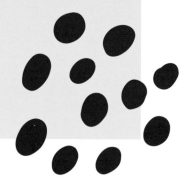

THE ONLY PERSON WHOSE APPROVAL YOU NEED IS YOU.

GO
WITH
YOUR
GUT

Your first instinct is often the right one. Learn to listen to your intuition and act accordingly. It's tempting to spend time overanalyzing and problem solving, but this can be mentally draining. Save your mental energy for the fun stuff by not overthinking, and have faith in yourself that if things don't turn out as favourably as you hoped, you'll find a way to work through it.

POSITIVE THINKING
WON'T LET YOU DO
ANYTHING; BUT IT WILL
LET YOU DO EVERYTHING
BETTER THAN NEGATIVE
THINKING WILL.

ZIG ZIGLAR

THINK POSITIVE

You can't choose what happens to you, but you can choose how you react. When things don't turn out as planned, there is always a lesson to be learned that will be useful in the future. And even on the worst days, there is usually at least one awesome thing to come out of it, if you know where to look. Get into the habit of writing down as many positive things that happened to you as you can remember at the end of each day. When you feel like times are tough, you can flick back through your notes and see all the glimmers of light that grace your day-to-day life.

LIVE LIGHT-HEARTEDLY

Sometimes it can help to get a bit of perspective. Our time alive is like a nanosecond in the long life of this planet, so try not to take yourself too seriously. Remember, the things that bother you today will be long forgotten in years, months or even by next week.

SAVOUR COMPLIMENTS

\\\\\\\\\\\\\\\\\\\\\\\\\\\\\\\\\\\

Do you find it hard to receive compliments and take them seriously? Do you tend to bat them away with a self-deprecating remark? You aren't alone, and it's a struggle for many people. But did you ever think about the fact that dismissing a compliment is actually a bit impolite? The next time someone makes the effort to pay you a compliment, try simply saying "thank you". Later, in a quiet moment, write the compliment down on a dedicated page in your journal. When you're feeling low, you can read back over the compliments to remind yourself of how awesome you are.

CHOOSE

HAPPINESS.

WE BECOME WHAT
WE THINK ABOUT.

EARL NIGHTINGALE

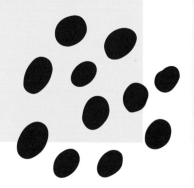

BELIEVE THAT YOU ARE ENOUGH.

TREAT
YOURSELF
RIGHT

Recognize your awesomeness by prioritizing acts of self-care. This can be a simple indulgence, such as treating yourself to a coffee in your favourite cafe, taking a leisurely aromatherapy bath or curling up with a good book. It can also mean taking good physical care of yourself by eating healthy, nutrient-rich food and exercising, or caring for your mental health by taking time out to relax and meditate (see page 148). Most importantly, it's about being patient, loving and gentle with yourself. It's about being your own best friend and treating yourself fairly and with integrity. It's about making time for self-care on a weekly basis, even when your schedule is super busy.

IT'S OK NOT TO BE OK

Every awesome person has off days, so cut yourself some slack. At times like this, remember that so far in life you have survived 100 per cent of your worst days. This too shall pass. Allow yourself to feel whatever emotions you're feeling, without judgement. Tomorrow is a new day and another chance to be awesome.

THERE'S NOTHING
EITHER GOOD OR BAD,
BUT THINKING
MAKES IT SO.

WILLIAM SHAKESPEARE

CHAPTER TWO:

EVERYDAY AWESOMENESS

Every day has the potential for awesomeness. Sometimes it can be as simple as taking time out to enjoy the little things in life. It's also about finding balance – doing more of what you love and spending less time on things that drain your energy. The same can be said for the company you keep – surrounding yourself with loving, supportive people is sure to fill your day with good vibes. Positive thinking will always see you through. Even on the darkest days there is something to be thankful for, if you know where to look. And never underestimate the power of small acts of kindness to add more joy to the world.

MAKE AN AWESOMENESS CALENDAR

What truly makes you happy? Make a list of the things you most enjoy doing in life. Include all the things you like to do to relax and unwind, whether that's gentle walks in the park, trips to the cinema, or something more active like playing your favourite sport. Now get out your calendar and factor in time each day for doing at least one of the things you love.

TRY SOMETHING NEW

Bring a sense of excitement to your daily life by challenging yourself to try something new each day. It could be something simple like ordering a different type of coffee than usual, taking a slightly different route to work or striking up conversation with a colleague you don't know very well. Perhaps you could try an activity for the first time – whether it's baking, belly dancing or base jumping, it will remind you that life is full of awesome new ways to enjoy living. It's normal to feel some level of fear when facing something new or unfamiliar. The more new things that you try, the easier you will find it to push through the fear that stands between you and new experiences.

DO MORE OF THE THINGS YOU LOVE.

" LEARN SOMETHING NEW. TRY SOMETHING DIFFERENT. CONVINCE YOURSELF THAT YOU HAVE NO LIMITS.

BRIAN TRACY

BE BRAVE ENOUGH TO BE BAD AT SOMETHING.

PRACTISE GRATITUDE

Make time each day to take note of and be thankful for something in your life. It could be a reliable friend, the flowers in your garden or simply the fact that you are in good health. Take a moment to sit down for five minutes and meditate about the thing that you are thankful for. As the days pass, you will have a growing sense of how awesome your life really is.

**"THANK YOU"
IS THE BEST PRAYER
THAT ANYONE
COULD SAY.**

ALICE WALKER

SMILE

Did you know that smiling releases endorphins? These are a group of chemicals also known as "happy hormones"! Studies have shown that a person's mood can change to match their facial expression. In other words, smiling can actually help cheer you up when you're feeling down. And seeing your smiling face might just lift the spirits of those around you, too.

EMBRACE JOMO

Social media makes it hard not to live life with a constant sense of FOMO – fear of missing out. But have you ever experienced JOMO, the joy of missing out? Sometimes it's far more satisfying to say "no" – those occasions when, deep down, you aren't all that keen on participating, but you go along with it to avoid feeling left out. Next time you're invited to a social event but it's cold and wet outside and you'd really rather spend the evening at home in your pyjamas hanging out with the cat, do yourself a favour and give in to the urge.

THERE IS
ALWAYS
A REASON
TO SMILE –
YOU JUST
NEED TO
FIND IT.

ENJOY THE LITTLE THINGS IN LIFE.

GET YOUR LAUGH A DAY

Scientific research has demonstrated that laughing can help to lower blood pressure, reduce stress hormone levels, improve cardiac health, release endorphins, boost the production of T-cells (which help you fight off sickness), increase general well-being and tone your abs. So as well as making sure you eat five portions of fruit and veg a day, ensure you get your daily dose of humour. Whether it's by watching an episode of your favourite sitcom, bingeing cat videos on YouTube or sharing funny memories with an old friend, make time to let loose, crease up and create some laughter lines you can be proud of.

FOR EVERYTHING YOU HAVE MISSED,

YOU HAVE GAINED SOMETHING ELSE.

RALPH WALDO EMERSON

CREATE A CIRCLE OF AWESOMENESS

Other people's energy can make a big difference to your own mood and outlook. After you spend time with a person, take a moment to perform an energy assessment – are you feeling uplifted and positive? Or are you feeling weary and drained? Surround yourself with people who amplify your own good vibes and limit the time you spend with people who take away your energy.

CHOOSE PEOPLE WHO
WILL LIFT YOU UP.

MICHELLE OBAMA

PAY SOMEONE A COMPLIMENT

Remember the compliments page in your journal (see page 37) and how good you feel when you read back over them? Why not spread the love and make someone else feel awesome by telling them how great they are – whether that's by admiring a friend's new haircut, praising a colleague for a job well done or letting your partner know how delicious their cooking is. By lifting others up, you will feel more positive, too.

GET IN TOUCH

Humans are social beings: we are fundamentally wired to seek out connections. That doesn't only have to be about making new friends, though. There is much joy to be gained (and shared) by reaching out to refresh existing bonds. Write a letter to an old friend you haven't seen in years, call or visit a relative who lives far away or send someone you love a present out of the blue. Hearing from you is bound to brighten their day.

MAKING PEOPLE FEEL GOOD FEELS GOOD.

PAY IT FORWARD

Has a stranger ever done
something kind for you, out
of the blue? Feels pretty good,
right? Remember that feeling
and find ways to spread it
to others in your daily life
– whether that's by buying
a homeless person a warm
lunch on a cold day, or giving
up your seat for someone on
the bus. It's long been held
that being kind to others can
boost your happiness, and
in 2016, a study undertaken
by the universities of Oxford
and Bournemouth in the UK
found that there is a solid link
between being kind to others
and our personal happiness.

CARRY OUT A RANDOM ACT OF KINDNESS, WITH NO EXPECTATION OF REWARD, SAFE IN THE KNOWLEDGE THAT ONE DAY SOMEONE MIGHT DO THE SAME FOR YOU.

DIANA, PRINCESS OF WALES

SIMPLE KINDNESS COSTS NOTHING BUT IS WORTH EVERYTHING.

**SPREAD JOY TO
THE PEOPLE YOU
ENCOUNTER EACH DAY,
AND IT WILL BE
RETURNED IN YOUR
LIFE TENFOLD.**

FREDRIK EKLUND

SHARE MESSAGES OF JOY

Look for opportunities in your daily life to share your awesome positive outlook with the world. You could write a positive quotation on the inside cover of a book, then give it away; leave a sticky note with an upbeat message inside an elevator; or write a happy thought for the day on a steamed-up mirror for your partner or housemate to read when they use the bathroom. By sharing good vibes this way, you increase the overall amount of positivity in the world and therefore the likelihood of some of it coming back to you when you need it most.

TODAY IS A GREAT DAY

TO SPARKLE.

GET OUTSIDE

Take some time out of your busy day to get outdoors and breathe in some fresh air. Time spent in nature is proven to raise our happiness levels – in fact, studies have shown that the benefits also include increased sleep duration, healthier blood pressure and heart rate levels and reduced stress.

NATURE IS THE BEST THERAPY.

UNLEASH YOUR CREATIVITY

Bring your imagination to life by making something each day – it could be baking cupcakes, doodling a spread in your journal or a simple DIY project, such as putting up a shelf. Being creative is fun and worth doing for its own sake, but it also has beneficial side effects. It helps you become a better problem solver because, instead of approaching things in a purely logical fashion, it allows you to see things from different angles. It can also make you better equipped to deal with uncertainty: creative thinkers are able to adapt to allow for the unexpected. Adopting this creative mindset will spill over into other areas of your life, helping you on your journey of personal growth to become even more awesome.

YOU CAN'T USE
UP CREATIVITY.
THE MORE YOU USE,
THE MORE YOU HAVE.

MAYA ANGELOU

WATCH THE SUNSET

/////////

Make it part of your routine to pause at the end of each day to enjoy the sunset. Turn it into a little ritual by making a calming beverage and settling in to a favourite comfortable spot to watch as beautiful colours fill the sky. This is an opportunity to be present in the moment, but also to reflect on everything that has been awesome about your day, and to be grateful for another 24 hours spent on our beautiful planet.

SLOW DOWN AND FOCUS ON THE DETAILS.

CHAPTER THREE

HOW TO BE AN AWESOME HUMAN

If you've read chapter one, you already know how awesome you are. You also probably realize that there is always room to grow — to learn from your mistakes and be open to new ideas. It's time to dig deeper into the top traits and values of an awesome human and work on enhancing them. Kindness, reliability, integrity, vulnerability, consistency and forgiveness all get a mention here. Remember that every action has the potential to spread positivity to the wider world, whether that's by being a good friend, by setting a good example or by helping others to see the funny side in a tricky situation.

TAKE ACTION

Now that you have a clearer idea of what awesomeness means to you, it's time to put an action plan in place to bring those qualities to the foreground. Using your mood board (see page 7) as a starting point, make a list of any qualities that you already possess. Next to each quality, write a behaviour or action that you feel manifests that quality – for example, if you write down "friendly", you might add "smile at strangers".

Make a second list of any qualities that you feel you are lacking or you would like to work on. Next to each, write down an action that you can take to manifest it in your life. Once you have a working list, you can get started right away on bringing these qualities into your daily life. Start small by picking just one and, for a week, find an opportunity to take the corresponding action each day. Before you know it, you will have formed an awesome new habit.

GIVE BACK

One sure-fire way to amplify your awesomeness is by finding ways to give back to the world. Think about how you could use your time and talents to benefit others. You could volunteer at a local charity, for example. There are many not-for-profit organizations that pair up younger people with senior citizens who live alone for weekly conversation and games meet-ups. Alternatively, you could become a mentor to young people starting out in your field of work. Find out which charities operate in your local area and sign up for a cause that means something to you.

YOUR GREATNESS LIES NOT IN WHAT YOU HAVE, BUT IN WHAT YOU GIVE.

SUCCESS ISN'T ABOUT HOW MUCH MONEY YOU MAKE; IT'S

ABOUT THE DIFFERENCE YOU MAKE IN PEOPLE'S LIVES.

MICHELLE OBAMA

LISTEN CAREFULLY

Listening with the intent to hear, rather than the intent to reply, is a very powerful communication tool. Next time you have a conversation with someone, try this: really focus on listening to what the person is saying, taking note of their tone of voice, facial expressions and any gestures they use. Be mindful of their vocabulary, and resist the temptation to jump in with your own thoughts when they pause. When having a conversation, especially a significant one, the most important thing you can give another person is your full, undivided attention – that will make you pretty awesome in their eyes.

SEEK FIRST TO
UNDERSTAND,
THEN TO BE
UNDERSTOOD.

STEPHEN R. COVEY

BE OPEN TO NEW IDEAS

An awesome person is always growing and learning. One of the ways in which you can open yourself up to new ideas is by mixing with people outside your usual social circle. A unique way to do this is to attend an event at a Human Library Book Depot (www.humanlibrary.org). Set up in Denmark in 2000, this organization "publishes" humans, organizing meet-ups so that other people can get together and "read" the "human books" by having a conversation with them. Each human on their bookshelves represents a group in society that is often subject to prejudice, stigmatization or discrimination due to factors such as their lifestyle, religion, ethnic origin and so on. You can ask questions and share ideas with someone with totally different insights on life than your own, and it's totally free! If you can't find a depot local to you, you can still visit a regular library to borrow books about – or written by – people from backgrounds and cultures other than your own.

LEARN TO FORGIVE

Accept others for who they are and remember that we all make mistakes. Holding on to anger and resentment after someone has harmed you or let you down will only cause you further pain, so learn to let go. Use this simple ritual to practise forgiveness and set yourself free:

1. Think of a person who you want to forgive. Close your eyes and really picture that person and how you feel toward them.

2. Visualize a black cord connecting you to that person. The black cord represents negative energy.

3. Imagine yourself cutting the cord and watching it disappear.

4. Now imagine a beam of white light connecting your heart to the other person's. It symbolizes good energy and connects you both as equals.

5. Say out loud: "I forgive you. Please forgive me. I love you. Thank you."

BE INSPIRED BY OTHERS

/////////

Who do you think is awesome? It could be a role model in your life, such as a teacher or older sibling. Think about what it is that makes them awesome – what qualities do they have to which you aspire? Or maybe there is someone famous you admire? Read about their life and achievements and how they got to where they are today. You may even realize that you share things in common.

BE
A
FORCE
FOR
GOOD.

**BE THE CHANGE
YOU WANT TO
SEE HAPPEN.**

ARLEEN LORRANCE

MAKE KINDNESS A HABIT

If we were kind to each other all the time, imagine what a happy world this would be. Practising kindness daily is very easy to do, and with each kind act you can be safe in the knowledge that you are making the world a little bit more awesome. Individual random acts of kindness are a great way to embrace this, but it can go much deeper. It could be that you adopt the kindness habit of making socially isolated people feel more included – for example, if you are at a social event and see someone alone hovering on the edge of things, go over with a warm smile, introduce yourself and encourage them to join in. It could also be the habit of being kind to yourself – not berating yourself when you make a mistake, for example. Once you start looking, you'll soon realize that the opportunities are endless.

ALWAYS BE KIND.

NO
EXCEPTIONS.

LEAD BY EXAMPLE

///////////////////////////

One of the principal rules of strong creative writing is "show, don't tell", and the same could be said of life – if you want to inspire others to do something, instead of telling them what they should or shouldn't do, just do it and show you are as good as your word. For example, if you care about the environment and are concerned about the impact of plastic use, you could work toward making all areas of your life plastic-free, from using reusable drinks cups to solid shampoo bars. Maybe you will inspire others to do the same!

SEE THE FUNNY SIDE

The next time something goes wrong, remind yourself and others that you will laugh about it in time. The most embarrassing moments in life make great material for funny stories to amuse your guests at your next dinner party, and holiday disasters that may at first seem dreadful are always the best anecdotes to tell when you get home.

YOU CAN'T REALLY BE
STRONG UNTIL YOU SEE A
FUNNY SIDE TO THINGS.

KEN KESEY

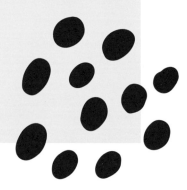

STAY CALM

Whatever situation you find yourself in, you can come out of it better by facing it with a cool and collected demeanour. If things get on top of you, take a few moments to stop and gather your thoughts. Close your eyes and bring your focus to your breath, inhaling and exhaling ten times. Now open your eyes and continue with focus and clarity.

JUST BREATHE.

BE CONSISTENT

///////////

Don't be afraid to stand up for yourself and others when your values are challenged. Don't change who you are or undermine your own values to fit in with other people. Be as good as your word – be the person who others can rely on to the best of your ability, and perhaps your consistency will inspire others to be just as reliable and supportive as you.

ALIGN YOUR ACTIONS WITH YOUR VALUES

Spend some time thinking
about what your key values
and moral principles are. Use
a journal or grab a pencil and
paper to note down any that
immediately come to mind,
for example kindness, honesty
or loyalty. Now look at each
value or principle and think
about actions you already take
to embody it in your day-
to-day life. Next, think about
other ways that you can bring
this value to the forefront of
your daily actions. Reflect
on what you've written and
return to your list regularly to
review it or make additions. By
being mindful of your values
in this way, you will gain a
stronger sense of self and
what really matters to you.

DARE TO LEAD.

> INTEGRITY IS DOING THE RIGHT THING WHEN YOU DON'T HAVE TO – WHEN NO ONE ELSE IS LOOKING OR WILL EVER KNOW.

CHARLES MARSHALL

ALLOW YOURSELF TO BE VULNERABLE

It's almost second nature
to want to protect yourself
by hiding your perceived
weaknesses and failings from
the world, but in doing so
you limit your ability to be
an authentic, multifaceted
being. It actually takes a lot of
courage to be open and show
your vulnerable side – you
will gain a lot of respect from
others, and self-respect, in the
process. You also demonstrate
to others that it's OK to
be vulnerable sometimes
and, through that example,
invite them to do the same,
paving the way for greater
openness and understanding
in your relationships.

VULNERABILITY IS
NOT WEAKNESS;
IT'S OUR GREATEST
MEASURE OF COURAGE.

BRENÉ BROWN

NEVER GIVE UP

If you try to do something and it doesn't work out right away, remember it's just a setback and not a failure. Some of the most successful people have faced many rejections before they could achieve their goals – J. K. Rowling was rejected by numerous publishers before she finally got a publishing deal for her Harry Potter books. The important thing is to keep on getting back up and trying again, to learn from your mistakes and keep striving toward your awesome future.

IF YOU DON'T GIVE UP, YOU CANNOT FAIL.

YOU ARE ALLOWED TO BE
BOTH A MASTERPIECE AND
A WORK IN PROGRESS,
SIMULTANEOUSLY.

SOPHIA BUSH

REMEMBER: IT'S A PROCESS

We are all works in progress; being awesome is something you have to work at every day. Take some time at the end of each day to reflect on how you acted and reacted in different situations that arose. For example, were there any moments when you allowed pessimism to creep in? Did you gossip about others? Did you behave in a passive-aggressive way? Write down the circumstances of what happened and how you could deal with the situation in a more positive way next time. Now note some moments where you felt good about the way you reacted in a difficult situation or showed kindness to others. Even if you've had a bad day, there is bound to be at least one. Give yourself a pat on the back for being awesome today.

EVERY NEW DAY IS A CHANCE TO BE BETTER.

CHAPTER FOUR

HOW TO LIVE AN AWESOME LIFE

You only live once. So how can you make your time on this planet as awesome as possible? It is often said that the key to happiness lies in living in the moment, in letting go of the past and not worrying about the future. So go ahead – pursue your passions, work toward your goals and do the things you have always dreamed of doing. Try new things, even if you're not that good at them – you'll never know until you start. But amid all this carpe diem, remember to take good care of yourself; to rest, reflect and consolidate all those happy memories you're making.

REST AND RECOVER

An important part of being awesome is looking after yourself, and that means listening to your body and making time to rest and recover when you need it. Find something that helps you relax – it could be taking a warm bath, visiting a spa, taking a gentle yoga class or simply lying out on a sun lounger all afternoon with a cool drink in your hand.

TAKE RISKS

If there is something you really want, go after it. Maybe you always dreamed of buying and renovating a house or starting your own business. You can spend a lifetime waiting to be ready to take the plunge, but the truth is no one is ever really ready. So stop waiting and take action now. Let go of the idea of perfect, embrace the opportunities in front of you and learn by doing. It might feel uncomfortable at first, but that's a good thing – getting out of your comfort zone is what enables you to change and grow into an even more awesome person than you already are.

DON'T ALLOW YOUR MIND TO TELL YOUR HEART WHAT TO DO.

THE MIND GIVES UP EASILY.

PAULO COELHO

INVEST IN YOURSELF.

FEED YOUR SOUL

Just as the body needs food and water to flourish, so too your soul needs sustenance in the form of beauty and inspiration. It can take many forms – be it visual art, music, literature or fine cuisine, or spending time in nature. Make time to get your regular fix and you'll soon be feeling awesome on a soul level.

ART IS SOMETHING
THAT MAKES YOU BREATHE
WITH A DIFFERENT KIND
OF HAPPINESS.

ANNI ALBERS

DO THINGS THAT BRING YOU JOY

Whatever you love to do, just do it — even if you're not perfect or even very good at it. For example, if you love painting but know you're no Van Gogh, you are still allowed to spend your money on art materials and your time on painting to your heart's content. Or perhaps there is an activity that you enjoyed as a child that you could revisit as an adult, such as ballet or making balloon animals.

LET GO

Whatever is weighing you down from your past – be it regrets about opportunities missed, relationships that ended badly or people who hurt you – let it go. Carrying resentment and grudges through life is only going to slow you down and take away energy that you need for doing the awesome things that you love. Try this simple ritual to find release: write down the thing you want to let go of on a piece of paper. You can write down as many as you like – just be sure to write each one on a separate scrap of paper. For the next part you will need a candle or open fire (since you're so awesome, we don't need to remind you to do this in a safety-conscious manner so as not to set fire to the house/your neighbour's pet). Now hold the piece of paper in your hand and say out loud: "I let you go", then drop the paper into the fire. Watch it burn, and the thing you've been holding on to disappear into the air with the smoke.

THERE IS GREAT POWER IN LETTING GO.

DARE TO DREAM

Is there something that you long to do, a once-in-a-lifetime experience that has always seemed a little too far out of reach? Dreams are what sustain us – they are the hope and fuel that keep us going even in the darkest times. So whatever yours is, be it climbing Everest, moving to Japan or winning an Olympic diving trophy, live your life as if anything is possible. Maybe you won't quite make it in the end, but along the way you could climb some smaller but still impressive mountains, learn Japanese or become part of a wonderful community of other aspiring divers. Or maybe you will make it and prove to yourself that anything is possible. There isn't any harm in trying.

THE MOST EFFECTIVE
WAY TO DO IT IS
TO DO IT.

AMELIA EARHART

RUN AFTER
EVERY
DREAM IN
YOUR
HEART.

"

JOY DOES NOT SIMPLY
HAPPEN TO US. WE HAVE
TO CHOOSE JOY AND KEEP
CHOOSING IT EVERY DAY.

HENRI NOUWEN

START RIGHT

Set yourself up for an awesome day with a morning routine. The great thing about having a routine is that it takes the stress out of mornings: following a set series of steps means that you don't have to do any decision-making. As well as the usual basics of eating a healthy breakfast, getting yourself dressed and checking you have everything you need before you leave the house, it could include some of the following:

- A morning meditation
- A short journaling session to set your intentions
- A workout or yoga session to get energized
- Spending some time in nature.

When you are forming your routine, don't get too hung up on the details: use your intuition and ease into what works for you. Consistency is key to routine, but don't be afraid to reassess after some time has passed and adapt anything that is no longer working for you.

NOURISH YOUR BODY

Being awesome all day every day takes a lot of energy, so make sure your body is getting filled up on the right foods to fuel your adventures. It's not rocket science, and you don't need a fad diet as long as you stick to the basics: drink plenty of water; eat lots of fresh fruit and veg, especially green veg; prepare healthy balanced meals that include a portion of veg, protein source and slow-release carb source; keep sugary snacks and fried and processed foods to a minimum and don't drink alcohol like there's no tomorrow. Back this up with regular heart-rate-raising exercise (150 to 300 minutes of moderate physical activity or 75 to 150 minutes of vigorous activity per week) and you're sorted.

NOURISH TO FLOURISH.

THE SECRET TO LIVING
WELL AND LONGER IS:
EAT HALF, WALK DOUBLE,
LAUGH TRIPLE AND LOVE
WITHOUT MEASURE.

TIBETAN PROVERB

BE SPONTANEOUS

Modern life can be regimented, with work deadlines, family commitments and social engagements all filling up the diary for months ahead. Every now and then it pays to be spontaneous and do something you feel like doing just for the fun of it – like instead of heading straight home at the end of the day, taking a more leisurely route past some beautiful scenery, dropping in on a friend for a cup of tea, or taking a loved one out for a surprise dinner.

THROUGH SPONTANEITY
WE ARE RE-FORMED
INTO OURSELVES.

VIOLA SPOLIN

LET
LIFE

SURPRISE YOU.

MEDITATE

Just like your body, your awesome brain needs a break every now and then. Take some time out of your day to meditate using this easy technique. Sit or lie in a comfortable position. Take some time to settle and close your eyes. Now simply focus on your breath. Thoughts will naturally pop into your mind, but the trick is to observe them and let them go, rather than letting yourself be carried away by them. If it helps you to focus, you can count the breaths in and out until you get to ten, then repeat. With even just five minutes of meditation a day you are bound to notice a difference.

TAKE SOME TIME TO CLEAR YOUR HEAD.

REDISCOVER A LOST TALENT

What are the activities that made you happiest when you were younger? Maybe you loved horse-riding, or you were an avid trainspotter or a nifty knitter. Reconnecting with old hobbies can be just as rewarding as starting new ones. Why not find a relevant local group or club to join? Having a regular meetup with likeminded folk is a fantastic way to get you motivated, and you might just make some new friends.

BEING PASSIONATE ABOUT SOMETHING MAKES YOU AWESOME!

SPEND YOUR TIME WISELY

Remember that your time is finite. Make the conscious decision to spend it doing the things that matter most – spending time with people you love, doing things you get pleasure from, nourishing your body and soul, working toward your goals. Protect your precious time and don't allow it to be used up by unfulfilling activities such as scrolling through social media or doing things that you don't enjoy to appease or please other people.

HELP IS ALWAYS AT HAND

Awesome people go through tough times, too. If you find yourself feeling low for two weeks or more, it is worth speaking to your doctor about it. They will be able to recommend something to help get you to a better place – whether that's a talking therapy such as CBT (cognitive behavioural therapy) or counselling, lifestyle advice, or medication. Remember: the doctor is there to help you, not to judge; tell them everything and that way they will be able to give you the best possible advice.

DO WHAT YOU CAN, WITH WHAT

YOU'VE GOT, WHERE YOU ARE.

SQUIRE BILL WIDENER

BELIEVE IN YOURSELF
AND YOU WILL BE ABLE
TO MOVE MOUNTAINS.

BINDI IRWIN

CONCLUSION

So you've come to the end of the book – congratulations! Hopefully you've learned a few tips and tricks that'll help you to maximize your awesomeness. Life's journey will always have its ups and downs, but by constantly looking for the positive in yourself, the world and the people around you, and being grateful for the things that you could easily take for granted, you will unlock the secret to a fulfilled, happy life.

Remember: make every day AWESOME!

If you're interested in finding out
more about our books, find us on Facebook
at **Summersdale Publishers** and follow
us on Twitter at **@Summersdale**.

www.summersdale.com